Dorchester
CENTURY

Dorchester CENTURY

STEVE WALLIS

DORSET BOOKS

First published in Great Britain in 2006

British Library Cataloguing-in-Publication Data
A CIP record for this title is available from the British Library

ISBN 1 871164 34 6
ISBN 978 1 871164 34 3

DORSET BOOKS
Official Publisher to Dorset County Council

Halsgrove House
Lower Moor Way
Tiverton, Devon EX16 6SS
Tel: 01884 243242
Fax: 01884 243325
email: sales@halsgrove.com
website: www.halsgrove.com

Printed and bound in Great Britain by
CPI Bath

Contents

Courtesy Maureen Attwooll

Bowling Alley Walk (looking west from the Trinity Street end), c.1905.

Acknowledgements

Among the many people I would like to thank for help in the production of this book are Mr K. W. and Mrs R. P. Barnes, John Bennett, Graham Bryant, Charles Cordy, Dennis Holmes, Gordon Le Pard, Simon Pomeroy, Andrew Price, Tony Jefferies, Mark Simons. Also the staff of the following bodies: the Dorset Local History Centre (particularly Robin Ansell); Weymouth Library (especially Nicola Brown) which holds the Herbert Collection of photographs; Came Down Golf Club; Kingston Maurward College (particularly Danny Bartlett); Dorchester Town Football Club; AC Archaeology (in particular Peter Cox); and Superdrug (especially Emma Young). Last and definitely not least, I must single out Maureen Attwooll for my particular gratitude for her invaluable assistance particularly concerning sources of photographs.

View north up West Walk dated 1904.

Looking west along South Walks, probably early twentieth century.

Introduction

This is a personal view from someone who has lived in Dorset for just over a decade and in Dorchester for most of that time. So, I have only seen changes over that period at first hand and have had to rely for the rest on written sources, photographs and information from others, but the perspective of an interested newcomer is not necessarily a bad thing.

I must also make an apology regarding the title of this book. Its topic is the twentieth century in Dorchester, but it cannot be confined exactly to that subject. There needs to be some overlap with the later nineteenth century and sometimes with earlier periods to put events and places into context, and it seems churlish to me to finish in 2000 when that was only a short time ago, so in some cases I have brought the story up to the present day. Also, I will look at the surrounding area since not only is it vital to the functioning of the town but also because the proximity of attractive countryside and villages that retain a lot of character add to the value of Dorchester as a place to live in or visit.

Someone once said to me that he saw Dorchester as the start of the West Country. This seems a fair statement to me, since it lies where a traveller heading west starts to encounter smaller rural towns and farms, with a lifestyle of a more relaxed pace than those they have left behind. This must be linked to a change in landscape not far west of Dorchester, where the open chalklands that are cut by broad river valleys (such as that of the Frome beside which Dorchester developed) give way to the more undulating landscape and smaller valleys of western Dorset that continue into Devon and Somerset.

Dorchester has been a county town for at least a thousand years, and has always been a market town for a wide rural hinterland. During the course of the twentieth century, it retained these functions, though with alterations to the details. The main change was its transformation into a tourist destination in its own right and as a base for those touring the surrounding countryside and the Dorset coast. This book attempts to show the changes and also what has stayed the same.

RIVER FROME, DORCHESTER.

Courtesy Maureen Attwooll

The River Frome at Dorchester. An Edwardian view that seems to be of the bend near the bottom of Friary Lane, looking west.

– 1 –
Physical Changes in the Town

*T*o the casual observer, Dorchester can seem timeless – a place that has changed very little in hundreds of years. In fact, it has been changing gradually all the time. It was fortunate to escape the damage caused by large-scale bombing during the Second World War, as happened to Exeter for instance, and the wholesale demolition of most of its centre for the building of a concrete shopping precinct, as happened to many towns in the 1960s and 1970s. It has shopping precincts, but they are relatively small and generally fit in with the rest of the town.

One of the most noticeable features of early pictures of the town is the lack of traffic on the streets. People out of necessity walked more, but also those who lived in surrounding villages still had their own village shops to go to. The limited number of consumer goods also meant that fewer deliveries were needed by town centre shops.

A view down High East Street with the Kings Arms on the left, c.1911.

Courtesy Dorset Local History Centre

When shopping in Cornhill and South Street, it is easy just to look at the modern fascias and interiors of the shops, which usually give the impression of a thoroughly modern building. However, look up and you often see evidence that the building is much older. Here are two photographs from 1956 and 1966 that show modern-style fascias coming into use.

Cornhill (northern end), 13/7/56. A view from the Corn Exchange to H. Samuel, a shop that is still there today.

Courtesy the Herbert Collection

Courtesy the Herbert Collection

View of Cornhill and the Town Pump, 28/6/66.

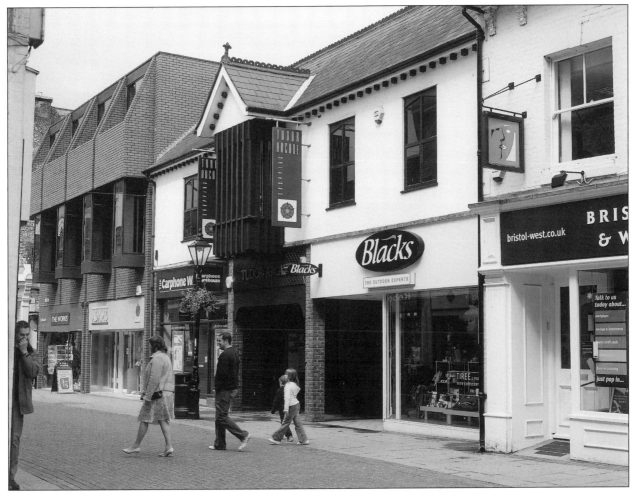

Tudor Arcade's frontage on South Street has been refurbished recently.

Tudor Arcade was built in 1957, a time when shopping arcades like it were very much in fashion. At that time, the building next to it and on the corner of Durngate Street was a Methodist church that had been built in 1875. This church was demolished in the early 1980s and the site redeveloped, and soon after the Waitrose supermarket was built at the end of Tudor Arcade on the site formerly known as Greyhound Yard.

Waitrose.

Here is a picture you may wish to bear in mind the next time you go down South Street so that you can compare it with the premises of JJB Sports that now occupies No. 14.

Hairdresser and wigmaker (H. W. Perham) at 14 South Street, c.1906.

A good example of care for historic architecture took place in the 1930s. A fourteenth-century doorway from a house in Colliton Street was re-erected inside the shop in South Street that today belongs to Superdrug. It can be seen inside that store on the right-hand wall.

The fourteenth-century doorway in Superdrug.

The Post Office.

At the south end of the pedestrianised part of South Street there is the Post Office. It is an impressive building that deserves a closer look than most of its users probably give the place. It was designed around 1904 by an architect called John Rutherford. The main materials used in its construction were red brick and Portland stone, and it has a variety of interesting architectural features, such as the Classical doorway and the green cupola on the top. The main entrance is on the corner, but there is a second, smaller entrance to the left. At the end of a short passageway that runs from this entrance there is a door that leads into the counters. There are two panels above that door that are dedicated to local Post Office staff killed in the two World Wars. Reflecting the higher casualty rate, the larger one (dedicated to eleven men) is that from the First World War. On the bottom right-hand corner it is dated September 1920 and has the name of its designer – Thomas Hardy.

The Grammar School and Napper's Mite.

Napper's Mite was built as ten one-storey almshouses for ten poor men under the will of Sir Robert Napper of Middlemarsh in central Dorset. The will stipulated the name Napper's Mite and dates from 1615. In the 1880s, the ten men in the almshouses each received a weekly allowance of 4s 6d. They shared a small area of land to cultivate and so provide more food for themselves.

In the twentieth century numbers declined, until in 1952 there were only three remaining residents. The almshouses were run by the Trustees of Dorchester Municipal Charities, and in that year they applied for permission to sell the building. Their proposal would have allowed any buyer to do as they wished, including demolishing the place. It was saved by Major John E. B. Duke, who bought and restored the building. He is said to have removed 600 tons of long-accumulated rubbish from the courtyard. Today the courtyard looks like it was originally intended, with two tall chimneys looming over it. In the former chapel of the almshouses, now the Napper's Mite Coffee Lounge and Licensed Restaurant, there is a stone tablet with the Napper coat-of-arms and an inscription to Sir Robert.

Dorchester's Grammar School was founded in 1569, but the building shown in the photograph was built in 1879 as a replacement. It was in turn demolished when the Hardye Arcade was constructed in the early 1960s. The arcade took its name from the Hardye School, an alternative name for the Grammar School.

Further down South Street past the Hardye Arcade is one of the two Goulds premises. The frontage is an interesting piece of late-twentieth-century design – it is built of brick with four projections, each triangular in section, above a little colonnade with brick columns.

The Hardye Arcade.

Southern Electricity Board show-rooms, 23/4/70. In Trinity Street, and now The Fire Station bar & club.

Goulds.

The junction, South Street, 19/11/1953. Looking east down High West Street from near Trinity Street junction (above).
Looking up South Street from junction with South Walks Road (below).

The sign of 'The New Inn'.

A little further along, near the end of South Street, there is evidence of one of Dorchester's lost pubs. Just below the roof line on the east side of the street there is a relief, whose style dates it to the early years of the century, with the words ' The New Inn' and the Eldridge Pope logo.

The Plaza Cinema is in Trinity Street. It opened in 1933 and its box-like structure is the best example of Art Deco architecture in the town. This was the 'modern' style of architecture at the time and so was very appropriate for a cinema, which, particularly since sound had been introduced into films only a few years before, was then the most up-to-date form of entertainment.

The Plaza Cinema.

All Saints' church, 27/5/60.

Courtesy the Herbert Collection

All Saints' church in High East Street is one of the landmarks of the town. The present structure is a rebuild of the 1840s. Like a number of other churches it was declared redundant, in this case in 1970, and it is now used as a store by the County Museum.

Architectural styles developed throughout the century, but there was also a growing consciousness of and respect for older buildings. Hence, by the end of the century older buildings were generally restored rather than replaced. A good example is the Antelope Walk shopping arcade off Cornhill. Developments of such arcades in earlier decades had begun with the demolition of whatever was already there, but in this case the early-nineteenth-century Antelope Hotel and its outbuildings were refurbished, and the room said to be the location where Judge Jefferies had tried the Monmouth rebels was converted to a tea-room that sees its historic connection as a selling point.

Looking down Cornhill from the entrance into North Square, c.1908.

Cornhill, a postcard sent in 1908. It includes the Antelope Hotel.

Cornhill, from the early 1920s. Note that the Antelope on the left now calls itself a garage.

The Trinity Street entrance to Antelope Walk.

The unchanged frontage of Antelope Walk today.

Two views of the Charles Street car park c.1966/67, one looking west with the Lock's Seeds store on the right (above), the other looking north.

Courtesy Mr K. W. and Mrs R. P. Barnes.

Courtesy Mr K. W. and Mrs R. P. Barnes.

There has long been a car park in Charles Street. It began on a small scale next to South Walks, on the site of a market. Then in the late 1960s it expanded to its present size, after the demolition of an old brewery building that had latterly become a store for Lock's Seeds. There were major proposals to redevelop the Charles Street site in the 1980s and 1990s, but to date nothing has come to fruition, and many local people hope that whatever is developed eventually will include a car park.

The Charles Street car park today.

The original County Hospital.

Much of the area behind Princes Street and Trinity Street is the former County Hospital site. A new hospital off Bridport Road was built in the early 1990s, and the residential redevelopment of the old site began later in that decade. As at Antelope Walk, the best of the old buildings were retained. Looking down Somerleigh Road, the main way into the complex from Princes Street, the large building to the left is the original hospital, dating from around 1840 and the work of Benjamin Ferrey, and the house facing in the distance is Somerleigh Court, built in 1885. As part of the redevelopment, a fountain was erected in Somerleigh Road on the site where the aqueduct that served the Roman town of Dorchester terminated.

The new fountain.

In the 1930s Dorset County Council, in common with other County Councils around the country at this time, decided to build itself a main administrative centre. It chose a site in Colliton Park, then the grounds of Colliton House. This was in the north-west corner of the town and had the advantages of proximity to the town centre and a lack of existing development.

The new County Hall was built in the years immediately before the Second World War, mostly using brick and with facings of of Portland stone.

Courtesy the Herbert Collection

Exterior view of County Hall, 26/5/56.

County Hall today.

Colliton House.

Colliton House itself was converted for use by the County Council. It dates from the sixteenth century, although much of what can now be seen from the outside is of eighteenth century date.

New developments have been added to the Colliton Park site over the years as needs have changed, including the new library that was built here in the 1960s.

New County Library HQ, 15/2/67.

The Borough Gardens next to West Walks were laid out in the 1890s, but there was a flurry of activity around 1905. That was the year of the dedication of the gaudily-painted clock tower, which has inscriptions on each face recording that it was presented to the Borough by Charles Hansford. Above the inscriptions are depictions of Hansford's head and the Borough Arms. The nearby bandstand was erected in the same year, and Hansford also paid for a fountain in memory of Alderman Gregory, who was instrumental in the original construction of the gardens. The fountain was restored in 1989 by the Dorchester Civic Society.

A view of the Borough Gardens from a postcard sent in 1906, showing the tennis courts and the clock tower only a year after it was dedicated.

Courtesy Maureen Attwooll

The Borough Gardens c.1920. The trees and shrubs are visibly lower than today, having only been growing for thirty years or so when this picture was taken.

The Borough Gardens – another early-twentieth-century view.

The bandstand today.

The Eldridge Pope brewery on Weymouth Avenue was a major local employer through most of the twentieth century. However, brewing ceased in the 1990s, although for a time the plant continued in use for the bottling of alcoholic drinks. The early twenty-first century saw plans for the site's refurbishment underway.

The Eldridge Pope brewery.

One of the glass-lined steel tanks (with a capacity of 3600 gallons) for making beer at the Eldridge Pope brewery – probably early 1930s.

The two railways that meet at Dorchester were in place in the nine-teenth century, so it might be thought that the only significant change of the twentieth century was the loss of steam trains. In fact, Dorchester South Station underwent considerable change. The original line from Southampton had stopped at Dorchester, and the station here had been built with a view to the line continuing westwards. When instead the line was continued to Weymouth, it had to curve away from the station before reaching it. Trains heading to Weymouth (the 'down' line) could use a new platform that was built at the time, but those on the 'up' line had to reverse into the original station.

This state of affairs continued until 1970, when construction of a new platform on the 'up' line meant trains no longer had to reverse into the old station, although the latter remained in use. In 1987 the present station building was constructed beside the 'up' line, and the old one was demolished soon after.

The Station pub at the entrance to Station Approach.

Courtesy the Herbert Collection

Dorchester South Station, 15/7/54. This shows track branching off into the station.

Dorchester South Station. The road in the foreground occupies most of the site of the old station. A former platform survives among vegetation just off to the left of this view.

The telephone exchange off South Walks was constructed in the late 1960s. Illustrating the pace of technological change, it became obsolete in the 1990s and was demolished to be replaced by housing.

Courtesy the Herbert Collection

New telephone exchange, Dorchester 2/8/68, shortly after its construction.

Dorchester has not shrunk from one of the more unpleasant aspects of its past. The junction of South Walks and Icen Way was once a place of public execution called Gallows Hill. In the 1980s a sculpture by Elisabeth Frink was erected here. It commemorates the 15 Dorset people who were executed on this spot for their religious beliefs, 14 of whom were killed between 1581 and 1594 during the reign of Elizabeth I. The sculpture has three bronze figures facing one another, suggesting a trial in progress. The central roundel on the ground between the figures has the words 'For Christ and conscience sake'.

The Dorset Martyrs sculpture, by Dame Elizabeth Frink.

Here is an interesting pair of views, looking both ways from the old Esso garage in London Road some fifty years ago.

Courtesy the Herbert Collection

London Road, Dorchester, 25/5/55.

Courtesy the Herbert Collection

The Trumpet Major.

This Victorian villa was converted into a pub in 1968, and has been extended since. As befitted its location on the Wareham road close to Thomas Hardy's home at Max Gate, it was given the name 'The Trumpet Major' after one of Hardy's novels. The name has recently changed to 'The Thomas Hardy'.

The Friary Press occupies buildings beside the Bridport Road a mile or so west of Dorchester. These buildings began life as part of the Dorchester radio station, which was opened by the Marconi Company on 16 December 1927. It was part of a network transmitting to New York, then South America, Egypt and Japan. Its beam aerials covered a wide area and must have been as prominent on the skyline as those at Rampisham are today. Technological changes meant the replacement of the beam aerials in the 1960s, and innovations such as satellite communications meant that the Dorchester station finally closed in April 1978.

The Friary Press. The two communications towers are modern and unconnected with the radio station.

Demolition of masts at Dorchester radio station on 16 April 1964. Quite an historic event is captured here.

CELEBRATING THE MILLENNIUM

This statue in Durngate Street is accompanied by a plaque that explains its origin and purpose. The sculptor was John Doubleday, and the work was commissioned to mark the year 2000 by Henry Ling Limited, printers of High East Street and a firm that has been associated with Dorchester for two centuries. To quote from the plaque, it is 'a tribute to the quiet heroism and wisdom and pastoralists and cultivators who provide inspiration to the literary tradition associated with Dorchester'. There is also a quotation from 'The Shepherd O' The Farm' by the nineteenth-century local poet William Barnes, who often wrote in Dorset dialect. Barnes and Thomas Hardy are the two best-known of the writers so stimulated. The statue's inspiration is a novel idea, and makes a good point about local culture – the local writers did not emerge from nothing, Hardy himself having an upbringing steeped in local rural life and basing many of his characters on people he had known.

'The Dorset Shepherd'.

– 2 –
Social Matters

$\mathcal{T}$his is a typical way that major events in the early twentieth century were celebrated, and there was nothing more important than the coronation of a monarch at that time. The event was taking place on the market site, I believe. Pictures of the ox were also taken before it was slaughtered. Today this may seem insensitive, and so I have not included any of them here, but people of the time clearly saw nothing wrong with it. In fact they were probably proud of the size of the beast they used to celebrate this event.

It is recorded that the first dish went to the Corporation, so perhaps things have not changed that much!

Ox being roasted to celebrate the Coronation of King George V, 22 June 1911.

'Roasting the Ox – Mr James Foot carving'.

Here is another way of celebrating in the early century. Mock-ups of a castle or tower entrance were placed across routes into the town for parades to pass through. This example sat across London Road where it crosses over the bridge near the White Hart pub and the junction with Fordington High Street.

A celebration in Dorchester.

Maumbury Rings has a long and continuing history of use for celebrations and other events, beginning several hundred years ago with public executions! This example is the Diamond Jubilee of Queen Victoria in 1897.

Courtesy Dorset Local History Centre

Maumbury Rings.

Market Day, Dorchester, c.1911.

Courtesy Dorset Local History Centre

Dorchester's main livestock market was moved from the area around Cornhill to a new site in Fair Fields in the mid nineteenth century, where it had advantages of more space and easier access to the newly-opened railway. Into the twentieth century the sale of livestock continued to be the main function, and there was also a livestock fair at Poundbury Camp.

Today, though livestock sales have stopped, there is still a thriving market on the site every Wednesday that attracts many people into the town. There is also a second-hand market on the site on Sunday mornings.

The Sunday market.

The decline in the number of pubs in the town is often mentioned by local people. This is common throughout the country and many Dorset villages have lost the pub that was once the focus of their social lives. There were around thirty such establishments in Dorchester at the start of the twentieth century, now there are about half that number. Those that have gone include the New Inn in South Street (the logo of which is illustrated in the previous chapter), the Dorchester Arms and the Half Moon in North Square, and the Star Inn in Icen Way.

The Swan, a former public house on the corner of Mill Street and Kings Road, Fordington.

The entrance to Mariner's Parade, High East Street. This was once the Three Mariners pub.

Fordington Hill, early twentieth century. Note the premises of Winzar & Sons in the left foreground, which were at a different location in 1903.

Courtesy Dorset Local History Centre

Today the vast majority of shops are in the town centre, with only a few elsewhere, most of which are 'corner shops' or mini-supermarkets. At the start of the century, shops outside the town centre were widespread and varied. For instance, those in Fordington in 1903 included Winzar & Sons, blacksmiths at 23 King Street, Samuel Wheeler, baker and grocer at 24 Mill Street, Thomas Soper, grocer in Holloway Road, a coffee tavern at 14 Fordington Hill, and Harry Dodge, baker, 48 Holloway Road.

The same view today.

Early-twentieth-century workers outside Lott & Walne.

Lott & Walne today.

In the latter years of the century, a number of industrial and other buildings were converted for residential use, notably around High East Street and the adjacent end of Fordington High Street. These included the former premises of Lott & Walne, which retains its attractive original frontage.

Courtesy the Herbert Collection

Dorset County Museum, St Peter's church and Town Hall. Edwardian period.

Courtesy the Herbert Collection

High West Street.

– 3 –
The Expansion of Dorchester

*T*he twentieth century saw a massive expansion of Dorchester's suburbs, a continuation of a process that had begun in the previous century. The Duchy of Cornwall owns much of the land on the south and west sides of Dorchester, and in the 1870s it began to sell some of this land off for development. One of the major developers was the Pope family, who built a brewery on part of the land, then amalgamated this with the Eldridge family's long-established brewing business to give Eldridge, Pope and Co.

The Popes began the Victoria Park development on former Duchy land in 1897. The roads were named after members of the Royal Family, such as Edward Road after the future Edward VII. Development was not necessarily as we think of it today, when once a site has planning permission work starts rapidly across the whole area. Instead, roads were laid out first, then houses built almost individually. For instance, Queen's Avenue was laid out in 1897 but five years or so later only four houses had been completed beside it together with a few more on the surrounding land, and much was still open hereabouts even after the First World War.

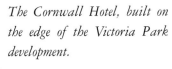

The Cornwall Hotel, built on the edge of the Victoria Park development.

Buses in Queen's Avenue, 10/8/70.

The proposed St Mary the Virgin church.

The Proposed Church of
S. Mary the Virgin,
Dorchester.

This Anglican church is in Edward Road within the Victoria Park development. It was built by the architect C. E. Ponting between 1910 and 1912. Compare the illustration above, which shows how the church was intended to look originally, with that below.

St Mary the Virgin church, as built.

This photograph was taken from a different angle to the illustration, since other buildings now obscure that view. The two are similar in many ways, but the major difference is that the tower was never built. However, look closely at the porch on the left of the building in the modern photograph and you will see massive buttresses that must have been built with the intention of supporting the tower. A lesser difference is the central spirelet shown on the illustration. Its base is there today, but the spirelet itself has either gone or was not constructed.

The following group of photographs give a good impression of what one area of Dorchester looked like before it was developed.

Two views of Weymouth Avenue, March 1956. These are taken from just past the cemetery.

Weymouth Avenue, June 1968. A view looking the opposite way to the previous two, taken from the vicinity of where the football ground is today.

The large-scale expansion of the town's suburbs continued through the century. Developments after the Second World War included the area around St George's Road and Eddison Avenue on the east side of Fordington and Castle Park on the south-west side of town. The latter was named from Maiden Castle, since it was an expansion in its direction. Expansion continued on the west side of town, out from the Victoria Park development and on both sides of the Bridport Road, with the area south-east of Poundbury Camp being built on in the 1960s.

Above: *St Mary's Catholic Primary School is a typical post-war school building. It was built in Dorchester's south-eastern suburbs, close to the site of the old Thomas Hardye school, and opened in 1966.*

Right: *Pummery Square – a completed part of the Poundbury development.*

Right: *An area of Poundbury under construction.*

The next bit of westward expansion involved the most famous housing development in the town, if not the county. A large area belonging to the Duchy of Cornwall was first earmarked for development in 1987, and plans were made according to the ideas and principles of urban design set out in the Prince of Wales' book *A Vision of Britain*, published in 1989.

The intention was to avoid the production of a sprawling characterless suburb, and instead to mix a variety of styles and types of housing with shops and commercial buildings, all of good quality architecture, to give more of an urban rather than a suburban feel. Individual buildings would each have the style of one particular historic period, and would be intermingled to give the impression of piecemeal building that can be seen in the historic centres of towns and villages that have not been damaged by uncaring modern development.

The proposals were and still are controversial. The development, which began in 1991 and will continue for some years yet, attracted national attention from the start, and debate is still going on. Some parts have been completed, such as Pummery Square, where there is the equivalent of a village hall in the Brownsword Hall, together with a variety of shops and a pub.

Other local developments in the 1990s had attempted to use traditional types, constructed sometimes with a mix of houses in the styles of different periods, sometimes with a more uniform thatched look. There are good examples in local villages such as Bradford Peverell and Stratton (see Chapter 9, 'Villages around Dorchester').

Dorchester's bypass had a major influence on the town in the later part of the century. Its construction was first considered in the 1940s, and a corridor along its proposed route was kept free of development for years before it was built. Work finally took place between July 1987 and October 1988 as a Department of Transport scheme from a new roundabout at Monkey's Jump on the Bridport road round the southern side of the town, with new junctions on the Weymouth and Wareham roads, for a distance of nearly 4 miles to the new Stinsford roundabout. At the same time, Dorset County Council constructed the Western Link road from Monkey's Jump roundabout down through Fordington Bottom to a new roundabout on the Yeovil road. This road was a mile and a quarter long.

More recently, the construction of a dual carriageway section of the A35 over Yellowham Hill in the early 1990s and the Puddletown and Tolpuddle bypass in the late 1990s improved Dorchester's road links.

Before the bypass was constructed, the A35, an important south coast road, had run straight through Dorchester along High West Street and High East

Street. This road was often blocked with traffic, and there was a very noticeable lessening when the bypass opened. It has built up again since then to some degree, though, partly because the bypass is of little value to traffic that is going from one side of the town to the other.

The bypass has also set a limit on the town's potential for expansion. For instance, the Fordington Fields development infilled an area within the south side of the bypass, and one of the boundaries of the Poundbury development is the section of the bypass east of the Monkey's Jump roundabout.

There was also some large-scale out-of-town development along Weymouth Avenue at the same time as the bypass was built. Dorchester Town Football Club gave up its ground in return for a new and better one close by, and a supermarket was built by Tesco with several other large stores close by. This development was not too large, and has not destroyed the shopping facilities of the town centre as has been alleged in cases elsewhere in the country.

Tesco's supermarket.

– 4 –
The Military

The Marabout Barracks was built by Poundbury Road in the eighteenth century. Then in the 1870s a new infantry barracks was constructed across Poundbury Road on a site that faced onto Bridport Road. Its gatehouse was built in 1876-7 in the style of a medieval castle, hence its popular name of the Keep. The Barracks, as it generally known, opened in 1879 and two years later became the depot of the newly-formed Dorsetshire Regiment.

The Barracks remained the base for the regiment for much of the century. In 1946 the regiment was honoured for its service in the recent World War and before with the freedom of the town, conferred at a ceremony at Maumbury Rings. Later it went through various amalgamations and changes, and now there is no military presence at the Barracks.

Courtesy Dorset Local History Centre

The Keep, c.1900 or slightly earlier. Here it is referred to as the 'Depot Gateway'. Some of the barrack buildings can be seen in the background. Note also the avenue of trees along Bridport Road, planted like others on roads leaving the town by Napoleonic prisoners-of-war. Some of this avenue was felled around 1900.

A military parade at the Barracks, c.1905.

Another parade of the same period.

However, today the Keep houses The Military Museum of Devon and Dorset, which contains displays on the history of the regiment and its successors and on military and wartime life in general. To the back, many other buildings of the Barracks also survive, but they are now used for other purposes, the Post Office's sorting depot being an example.

The Keep.

The Barracks.

The First World War saw a massive increase in the size of the Army, with many recruits needing training before being sent to the front. There was a correspondingly large expansion of the Army presence in Dorchester. The existing barracks could not accommodate all the new recruits and many slept in tents on open fields out to the west of them. (Much of this area has since been covered by housing and industry as Dorchester has expanded.) The recruits' training included the digging of trenches, and some backfilled examples of this period have been found on the site of the new Poundbury development. What looks at first glance like a rather incongruous and substantial brick wall in the valley bottom just below Poundbury Camp and next to the railway line is a remnant of a contemporary rifle range used for military training purposes.

The rifle range below Poundbury Camp.

Courtesy Dorset Local History Centre

'Hauptansicht des Lagers in Dorchester.' *It is a general view looking down the slope from the rampart of Poundbury hillfort.*

Courtesy Dorset Local History Centre

'Die Ankunft der Morgenzeitung' – that is, the arrival of the morning newspaper.

A matter of concern when the war began was the presence in this country of German citizens and others who were considered a potential threat to national security. Some of these from the local area were kept within the area used by the Army, and were soon joined by German prisoners-of-war. A dedicated camp for these prisoners was then established on the sloping ground just east of Poundbury Camp, where there is now an industrial estate. The prisoners-of war were used as labourers in the town and on surrounding farms, becoming a common sight as they marched through the town to their work. They were also taught English and allowed their own entertainments, keeping communal pets and having a makeshift theatre, for instance.

Courtesy Dorset Local History Centre

'Die Musikkapelle in Kasernenhof' – the band in the Barracks' yard.

The German memorial in Fordington cemetery.

The War Memorial.

A memorial to the German prisoners of the First World War who died whilst in captivity in Dorchester can be found in Fordington cemetery, which can be reached from behind St George's church. A German soldier is depicted in prayer, and there is an inscription in German which translates as 'Here rest German soldiers, not forgotten though in foreign soil'. The memorial is cut into ground below the main cemetery that drops away towards the River Frome; it is best seen looking up from the adjacent part of Holloway Road.

In common with just about every town and village in the country, when the First World War, or Great War as it was known then, had ended, Dorchester erected a memorial to its dead. It was set up in South Walks near the junction with South Street, and was unveiled on Empire Day 1921. The makers were Messrs Grassby and Son, the same firm of stonemasons that had worked on the Keep in the 1870s.

Courtesy Dorset Local History Centre

Here are comparative views of the same section of South Walks both taken around 1905. Note the well-known Victorian hexagonal postbox on the left in both views that is still there today, but of course the War Memorial has not yet been erected.

South Walk, Dorchester.

Courtesy the Herbert Collection

The Second World War also had an impact from the very start. In 1939 it was believed that any war would begin with an immediate and heavy bombing of major cities, and contingency plans were made to deal with this threat. Hence, over the weekend in September of that year when war was declared, nearly four thousand women and children were evacuated to Dorchester. Most soon went back when the immediate threat was not as bad as expected, but other people were evacuated here over the course of the war, including soldiers recuperating after Dunkirk.

Early in the war, various measures were taken to protect the country from German invasion. Some of the most visible remains of this activity that survive today are pillboxes, small fortified emplacements, generally made of concrete or brick, that would enable defenders to protect strategic locations. The two illustrated here are both on the south side of the River Frome beside roads that crossed the river, and so must have been intended to protect those crossings from invaders who had landed on the coast.

A pillbox near Tincleton.

A pillbox near West Stafford. It is now almost covered by vegetation, but some brickwork is just visible.

We generally think that after the Battle of Britain, Germany's plans for the invasion of Britain were forgotten as Russia became Hitler's new target. However, a 1941 plan involved landings in several places, including parachutists being dropped into the countryside between Dorchester and Weymouth who would then link up with seaborne invaders.

Another myth is that everyone 'mucked in' together because of their shared fighting spirit. In fact, Dorset like other places has stories of difficulties between evacuees and those on whom they were billeted – sometimes the evacuees were from 'problem families', sometimes their hosts were unwelcoming. Others rebelled against wartime regulations and laws, such as the Dorchester man who was fined by Bow Street magistrates in London for not selling his personal objects of gold to the Treasury as all were required to do.

It is right to balance this by pointing out that most people 'did their bit'; for instance, a group of ladies chaired by a Miss Chadwick of Queens Avenue organised collection of aluminium for aircraft construction.

As part of the preparations for the invasion of Europe that was to begin with the D-Day landings in Normandy in June 1944, Dorset was a major centre for the build-up, much of it as low-key as possible as the intention of the Allies was to fool the Germans into believing the invasion would come from around Kent to the Calais area. Dorset was within the western part of the area where the invasion forces built up, and this part was predominantly that of the Americans. Weymouth and Portland were the main locations from which the D-Day troops would depart.

The United States 1st Infantry Division was billeted in Dorset from November 1943, including some in the Barracks and others elsewhere in Dorchester, with others camping in the countryside around the town. Kingston Maurward was even requisitioned as a petrol storage depot!

– 5 –

Archaeology

$\mathcal{A}$ section ostensibly dedicated to prehistory and early history may seem out of place in a book on the twentieth century. However, the century saw big advances in knowledge of the past and the ways in which ancient remains were studied and treated, and many of these changes can be seen operating in the Dorchester area.

The town already had a good record in protecting its heritage, notably during railway construction in the mid-nineteenth century. The builder of

The Nine Stones, Winterbourne Abbas, 30/6/65. The countryside around Dorchester has many nationally-important archaeological sites, such as this prehistoric stone circle that lies just west of Winterbourne Abbas beside the A35 main road.

Courtesy the Herbert Collection

the Bristol to Weymouth railway line, Isambard Kingdom Brunel, was persuaded to tunnel under the Iron Age hillfort of Poundbury Camp rather than cut through it and to redesign its junction with the existing line from London and Southampton in a way that preserved Maumbury Rings.

On the subject of Maumbury Rings, a good example of important archaeological work in the early twentieth century is the excavation of that site directed by H. St George Gray from 1908 to 1913. This has remained crucial to the understanding of how the site developed to this day. The excavator knew he was investigating a Roman amphitheatre before he started, but the work was to show that the Romans had reused a henge monument that dated from about 2500BC in the late Neolithic period. It also showed details of how the site had functioned as an amphitheatre, with two phases of use, the first probably by the Roman army, the other by the civil population of the town. The work also explained how the site was remodelled by Parliamentary forces during the Civil War, functioning as an artillery fort between July 1642 and June 1643.

MAUMBURY RINGS, REMAINS OF ROMAN AMPHITHEATRE, DORCHESTER.

Courtesy Maureen Attwooll

Maumbury Rings, early years of the twentieth century.

Maumbury Rings, looking north-east.

Maiden Castle c.1924.

Another major excavation linked the Dorchester area's most impressive ancient site, Maiden Castle, with arguably Britain's most famous archaeologist of the twentieth century, Sir Mortimer Wheeler.

In the early 1930s Wheeler had just completed a major excavation campaign in and around the Roman town of Verulamium, the modern St Albans. When he expressed his intention to excavate at Maiden Castle, in the words of his biographer, 'Archaeologists expressed no surprise, for it was held to be obvious that no other site was large enough, or challenging enough, to satisfy Mortimer Wheeler at this vaulting stage of his career'.

The western end of Maiden Castle.

Around 100 assistants, students and volunteers worked on each of his excavation seasons, during the summers from 1934 to 1937. Wheeler stayed at the Antelope Hotel and the excavators often socialised in Dorchester – they must have been a familiar sight around the town at the time.

Wheeler had a flair for publicising the results of his work, to the extent that some considered that he 'aimed more for literary than scientific values' in his reports. Be that as it may, *The Times* ran an article on the excavation every year that it was in progress, while Wheeler staged press days once a week. The work was sometimes filmed and a colleague even went to London to talk about the dig on the BBC's fledgling television service. The excavation report was published in 1943, and Wheeler went on to become a panellist on the television programme 'Animal, Vegetable or Mineral' in the 1950s.

In the grounds of County Hall there is the Roman Town House, which is the only complete urban Roman house on display in Britain. While most previous archaeological work had been for research purposes or simple antiquarian interest, it was found during one of this country's earliest examples of rescue archaeology – the excavations directed by Lt Col K. D. Drew, Curator of Dorset County Museum, and K. C. Collingwood-Selby in 1937 and 1938 in advance of the construction of County Hall. They expected to

The Roman Town House, general view.

The west range and its cover building.

find Roman material, since the site was known to be in the north-west corner of Dorchester's Roman town. Find it they did, including evidence that in Roman times most of the area had been used for industrial purposes, but the good condition of what became known as the Town House and its features, such as mosaics and a well-preserved window, was a surprise.

When the significance of the building was recognised, the plans for the new County Hall were changed so that it could be preserved and displayed. However, ideas of a cover building were shelved because of changed priorities with the start of the Second World War and the site, mosaics and all, was left uncovered until about 1950. Around this time, the upstanding walls were consolidated and the mosaics and other floors were covered with turf to protect them. One mosaic alone was left on view, covered by a small shed-like structure and visible through a glass panel.

In the late 1990s the County Council decided to redisplay the site. There are two ranges of rooms on the site, of which that known as the west range had the better features and must have been the household area. The south range included rooms of a more industrial function. The mosaics and floors of the western range were uncovered and conserved and a cover building built over that range. This was designed to give an impression of the original Roman building while being recognisably modern. The southern range gives a good idea of what the west looked like before the cover building was constructed.

The south range of the Roman Town House with a well in the foreground.

Attitudes to archaeology have changed, and about what deserves to be protected and what constitutes protection for remains. For instance, in the early 1970s it was considered perfectly acceptable to build an industrial estate right up to the ramparts of Poundbury Camp, the Iron Age hillfort, which was then as now given the status of a Scheduled Ancient Monument (a recognition that it is nationally important). An archaeological excavation took place ahead of the development and revealed, amongst other things, an important Roman cemetery, but there was little or no general outcry against the development. Undoubtedly the main thing in people's minds was that the town needed an industrial estate and here was a space for it that was conveniently close to the town and main roads.

Today when environmental and related issues are given much greater prominence, it is probable that such development would be considered as damaging to the setting of Poundbury Camp, so it would almost certainly not have been built so close to the rampart, and there would be concern about the effect on the cemetery too.

A late Roman stone coffin found in the excavation on the Poundbury industrial estate that is now on display beside the Roman Town House.

Other excavations have taken place in the Roman town. In 1978, for example, a part of the Roman baths was recorded ahead of construction of a car park in Wollaston Fields. The remains were covered and protected before development, and many local people, especially those who visited the site, still debate whether the remains should be re-exposed and displayed.

Wollaston Fields car park.

Then in the early 1980s more excavation took place on the site of the former Methodist chapel and at Greyhound Yard ahead of development. Some of the results were used to enhance the new development, with a series of interpretative panels set up outside the new Waitrose supermarket and the locations of the posts of a Neolithic monument marked out in the basement car park.

The panels outside Waitrose.

The Roman aqueduct can be seen as a terrace along this hillside west of Poundbury Camp.

Erosion repairs on the south-west corner of Poundbury Camp.

Work carried on elsewhere, too. In the mid-1980s English Heritage carried out more work on Maiden Castle to help in its long-term management. Construction of the Dorchester bypass was preceded by extensive excavation that yielded a wide variety of evidence. By the 1990s Bill Putnam was finding the true source of the Roman aqueduct that served Dorchester and understanding how it worked by selective excavation, and around the turn of the century the Duchy of Cornwall was working with Dorset County Council and English Heritage on the management of earthwork sites such as Poundbury Camp and sections of the Roman aqueduct. Developments in the town took increasing account of archaeology and much of the former County Hospital site was developed in a way to avoid disturbance of Roman levels, with excavation taking place only where necessary.

Poundbury Camp and the aqueduct seen from the Yeovil Road.

A prehistoric henge monument excavated at the Dorchester Middle School in 1998 by AC Archaeology.

– 6 –
Thomas Hardy

*T*homas Hardy is undeniably the most important person associated with the arts in Dorchester's history. He lived from 1840 until 1928, and though all his novels were written during the nineteenth century and the poetry to the writing of which he turned in the twentieth century is less recognised today, he still had a major influence on the area during the latter century.

Thomas Hardy's birthplace is in Higher Bockhampton, at the end of the lane that runs through the hamlet, just before the start of what was then Hardy's Egdon Heath. It was very much the family home, being built by Hardy's great-grandfather in 1800. The novelist was born here on 2 June 1840, and wrote his early novels in his room upstairs. The place now belongs to the National Trust and is little changed today. The roof is

Thomas Hardy's birthplace – an early view that must have been published around the time of Hardy's death.

Courtesy Maureen Attwooll

thatched and the walls are made of brick, stone and cob, with lots of evidence of repairs over the years. Inside the rooms are made to look as closely possible as they did when Hardy lived there. So it can be visited as the sort of shrine to a famous person that became increasingly common during the twentieth century or an example of nineteenth-century Dorset rural life.

Despite his literary success, Thomas Hardy continued to work as an architect. Below is Talbothayes Lodge, just east of West Stafford, that he designed as a home for his brother Henry in the 1890s. Their sisters Mary and Kate also moved in and lived here until their deaths several decades into the twentieth century. Henry was something of a local character and was often seen driving around the countryside. Talbothayes Cottages are across the road from the Lodge and are probably also Hardy's work.

Talbothayes Lodge.

Sales of his books brought him a good income, and in 1885 Thomas Hardy designed a new house for himself. Called Max Gate, it is on the edge of Dorchester off the Wareham road.

During his occupancy of Max Gate, Hardy became closely involved in the life of Dorchester. He was often seen walking into town, and acquired a reputation of being grumpy (perhaps not surprising to those who have read his novels!). He was passionate about the antiquities of the area and involved himself in campaigns to save them – Medieval parish churches in particular. Here is one example.

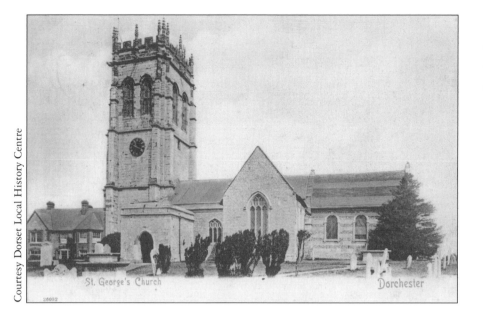

*St George's, Fordington c.1904
– a view before the extension was
added.*

In 1898 it became clear that St George's church in Fordington needed considerable repair and discussions began on what to do. These were given added impetus when on 12 February 1901 a storm sent a pinnacle off the tower through the church roof. The next year the pinnacles on the tower were replaced and other works took place, including the addition of an octagonal finial on the tower.

Hardy was a member of the restoration committee, but resigned in disgust when he returned from a holiday to see this new finial, which was architecturally incorrect and which others also disliked. (You can see it today if you go around to the north side of the tower.).

*A modern view of the elongated
St George's church, Fordington.*

In 1906 the Rev. Bartelot of the church and a parishioner architect J. Feacey planned an extension to the nave and a new chancel. Work on the nave ran from 1907 to 1911, and in 1908 they found the Roman tombstone that is still on display inside the church. Work on the chancel did not start until in 1914 and was interrupted by the First World War.

When Thomas Hardy died on 11 January 1928, his reputation was already such that the ashes of most of his body were buried in Poets Corner in Westminster Abbey. However, his heart was buried in the churchyard at Stinsford (this being the parish church of Higher Bockhampton where he was born) as a symbol of his attachment to the area. The churchyard lies a mile or so east of Dorchester, and is well worth a stroll out from the town across the watermeadows of the Frome.

Hardy's heart and other family graves in Stinsford churchyard.

The heart was interred with the body of Hardy's first wife, Emma Lavinia Gifford, and in 1938 the body of his second wife, Florence Emily Dugdale, was also buried there. The tomb is among the graves of other members of the Hardy family – beside it is the grave of Hardy's three siblings, Henry, Mary and Kate. Their parents' grave is on the other side and there are other Hardys of their generation and older close by. In 1972, Cecil Day Lewis, a poet laureate, was buried nearby as a mark of his respect for Thomas Hardy.

After his death, a lot of Thomas Hardy's papers were bequeathed to Dorset County Museum, so that it has become a centre for study of the man and his work. Displays on the author in the museum include his study, recon-structed here from Max Gate.

Dorset County Museum.

The American monument to Thomas Hardy.   *The statue of Thomas Hardy.*

At the junction of paths beside Hardy's birthplace there is a column that demonstrates how rapidly and widely the 'cult' of the man spread. It was set here only three years after Hardy's death, and according to its inscription it was '...erected to his memory by a few of his American admirers'. Appropriately for such a transatlantic memorial to a man whose work has been the subject of much academic study, it was unveiled on 16 April 1931 by a Professor J. Livingstone Lewes who belonged to both Oxford and Harvard Universities.

In the same year as the American memorial was set up, a statue of Thomas Hardy was erected in Dorchester itself. This is in a prominent spot on West Walks near the Top O'Town roundabout. It is the work of the sculptor Eric Kennington, and was unveiled on 2 September 1931. Today many tour groups, including those from all over the world who visit on specialist tours devoted solely to Hardy, can be seen admiring it.

It is ironic that the man who recorded the old market town of Dorchester and the surrounding rural landscape was one of the main reasons for its change to a tourist centre.

– 7 –
Tourism and Leisure

The museums and displays built up by the World Heritage company in Dorchester over the latter part of the twentieth century are aimed at visitors and demonstrate the importance of tourism to the local economy. By the century's end there were three attractions, the Tutankhamun Exhibition in High West Street, The Teddy Bear Museum in Antelope Walk and the Dinosaur Museum in Icen Way.

The Tutankhamun Exhibition.

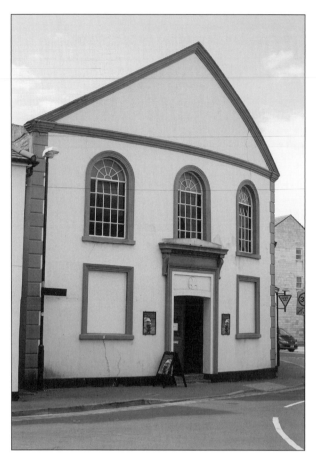

The Terracotta Warriors Exhibition.

The Baptist chapel – an Edwardian view. Note the date of construction, 1830, on the frontage.

The Tutankhamun Exhibition is housed in a building with a rather unusual history. It was constructed as a church in Wareham in 1889, where it was called St Michael's, and was taken down and rebuilt stone-by-stone on its present site in 1906-7, where it served Dorchester as a Roman Catholic church. It was replaced in this rôle by Holy Trinity church across High West Street in 1976.

The three were joined in the first years of the twenty-first century by the Terracotta Warriors Exhibition at the bottom of Fordington High Street. The latter is housed in a building that had previously been the Kingdom Hall of Jehovah's Witnesses, and that had started out as a Baptist chapel. The two photographs show the building's first and third functions.

Today the Judge Jeffreys' restaurant is well-known in Dorchester, and is a stop on the tourist trail because of its association with the infamous seventeenth century judge who stayed here while trying the Monmouth rebels. It was only around 1930 that it was given this name, and these two earlier photographs show it as just another business premises.

Judge Jeffreys', c.1905. The place was a Clothing and Outfitting Store.

Judge Jeffreys', 1920s. This pre-dates the 'tourist' association with the Judge. It now belonged to a leather merchant. Note the unrestored frontage of the almost equally historic property on the right that today belongs to Mabb & Sons.

DORCHESTER TOWN FOOTBALL CLUB

Dorchester Town Football Club was founded in 1880 at a meeting at the King's Arms public house and so celebrated its 125th anniversary in 2005. In the 2004/5 season the club reached its highest ever point in the league, just missing out on the playoffs for the Nationwide Conference South.

Through the twentieth century the team played in an assortment of leagues, with 'glory days' in the 1950s when it reached the 'proper' rather than qualifying rounds of the FA Cup five times, playing teams like Norwich City and York City. The achievement was repeated in 2000/1, when Dorchester Town played Wigan Athletic in the first round of the competition.

In the late 1980s the club's old ground became the site of the Tesco supermarket, and in return the club got the new Avenue Stadium next door. It is considered one of the best grounds for a club at this level.

The Avenue Stadium.

CAME DOWN GOLF CLUB

This is a prominent feature on the Ridgeway that separates Dorchester from Weymouth. Even if you can't always see it directly from Dorchester, you sometimes see sunlight reflecting from car windscreens in the car park there! It was constructed in 1896 as a nine-hole course for what was then the Dorchester golf club. The turn of the century was a time when golf was enjoying increasing popularity, and Weymouth Town Council wanted a course of its own. Unable to find a suitable site, it got involved at Came Down, and between 1904 and 1906 the course was extended to its present 18 holes to a design by a professional golfer. A small station was even built near Winterborne Monkton on the railway line between Dorchester and Weymouth just to serve the course. It opened in 1905 and closed in 1957.

Came Down Golf Club 17/9/55. Looking uphill towards Came Wood and the clubhouse.

Courtesy the Herbert Collection

A view looking north down the course with Dorchester in the background.

Three famous golfing brothers – Ernest, Charles and Reg Whitcombe – had strong associations with the Came Down club. These began in 1910, when the eldest, Ernest was appointed club professional – he was then only nineteen. His brothers soon joined him and developed their careers here, with a break for service in the First World War.

They were noticed just after the war by Samuel Ryder, a Hertfordshire businessman who liked to spend his holidays at Weymouth and play golf at Came Down. Ryder saw them as an example of the lack of opportunities available to young British golfers in comparison with their American counterparts, and decided to set up challenge matches between British and American golfers, the first of which took place in Scotland in 1921. For the next match five years later he donated a trophy in his own name, and thus was the Ryder Cup born.

The Whitcombe brothers moved to other clubs in the 1920s, and between them they played in the Ryder Cup ten times. Reg also won the Open in 1938.

With increasing leisure time available to people as the century progressed, the countryside became valued more and more as a place of recreation. Places such as Thorncombe Wood, the nature reserve a couple of miles east of Dorchester, became popular, and long-distance trails for walkers and sometimes riders were formed. A local example in the Jubilee Trail, established in 1996 by the Ramblers' Association. Its 90-mile course through Dorset takes it through the countryside south of Dorchester, past the Hardy Monument, Upwey, West Knighton and Moreton.

Thorncombe Wood.

– 8 –
Landscape

It became increasingly difficult to support large houses and their grounds as private residences alone, particularly with increased taxation after the Second World War. Here are some examples of local houses that have changed and survived.

Athelhampton lies between Puddletown and Tolpuddle on the now-bypassed section of A35. The hall was built in the late fifteenth century by Sir William Martyn, who became Lord Mayor of London, and was extended in the following century. Its formal gardens were laid out in the 1890s.

Through the twentieth century it had a series of caring owners who in many cases conserved and improved the house and gardens. It is open to the public and hosts wedding receptions and other events.

Athelhampton Hall near Dorchester, c.1906.

Wolfeton House c. 1934.

Wolfeton House is a fine example of a Tudor manor house that lies just south of Charminster, overlooking the water-meadows of the Frome valley. It was built by the Trenchard family, notably Sir Thomas and his great-grandson Sir George, with work taking place throughout the sixteenth century. Wolfeton House was formerly the manor house of a separate settlement of Wolfeton, which has long since disappeared except for the house and its grounds. Like Athelhampton, it is open to the public, in this case on particular days over the summer. A Tudor riding house, a long barn-like structure in which horses could be exercised away from the elements, nearby formerly belonged to Wolfeton House and may be the earliest example of such a feature in this country.

While some country houses such as Athelhampton and Wolfeton have just opened to the public and hosted events, others have gone through more drastic changes to survive.

A good example is Kingston Maurward House, which lies about a mile east of Dorchester within its extensive grounds. It is on high ground and if you stand in the town near the Corn Exchange and look along High East Street, it can be seen on the skyline. The House was built in the 1720s by one George Pitt as a replacement for a smaller Tudor building that still survives within its grounds under the name of the Old Manor House.

The estate stayed in the Pitt family until the mid-nineteenth century, then went through several changes of ownership over the next hundred years. One of the owners was Sir Cecil Hanbury, who possessed it from 1914 until his death in 1937. He became the Member of Parliament for North Dorset, during which time the house was often visited by Cabinet Ministers, foreign royalty and Thomas Hardy, who was a friend of Sir Cecil. Ten years after Sir Cecil's death, Dorset County Council bought the place and its grounds from his widow, Lady Hanbury, for the sum of £24,000, with the intention of using it as a Farm Institute, i.e. a centre for the teaching of agricultural and related skills. The place was in some disrepair, and Dorset County Council had to spend a further £20,000 on restoration before it could be used for its intended purpose. The American government also chipped in, to make up for any damage caused when its Army had used the grounds for petrol storage during the preparations for D-Day.

The range of courses offered expanded over the years and in 1993 the College, like all Further Education Colleges, became independent of its Local Government parent body, the County Council. It has diversified into a conference, meeting and wedding venue, and visitors are attracted by its gardens and animal park. A terrace on the south side of the house that gives fine views across the ornamental lake is the scene of an annual spectacular display of fireworks every 5 November, to which it seems that most of Dorchester troops or drives out.

Kingston Maurward House from its gardens.

The heathland east of Dorchester has often been seen as a wilderness. Thomas Hardy called it 'Egdon Heath' and his descriptions of it have helped this view. It is actually part of a much more extensive tract of heath that once extended to Dorset's eastern border and beyond, and it was actually a source of many people's livelihoods, with livestock being grazed on it and gorse and the like being gathered for fuel. Inroads were made into it before and during the twentieth century, with areas being taken in for agriculture, as has happened to much of the area south of Moreton.

Moreton Heath.

Courtesy Dorset Local History Centre

Sheep at Hardy's Monument 26/11/79. Grazing by livestock, and sheep in particular, was essential to maintain the downland that formerly covered most of the chalk hills of Dorset.

Around the middle of the century Government policy saw production of timber in this country as a priority, particularly so that the country would not be dependent on imports, particularly after the experiences of the two World Wars. Hence, owners of heathland were encouraged to plant trees, turning much of the high ground east of Dorchester into a landscape of conifers. Late in the century, an increasing understanding of the value of heathland for nature conservation, plus its attractiveness as a landscape and resultant interest to tourists, caused a reverse in official thinking, and owners are often give incentives to restore heathland. Both the tree planting and heathland restoration were entirely logical at their times, but many landowners remain amused by the apparent contradiction.

Dorset has a strong survival of old landholding patterns that date back at least to the Middle Ages, most noticeable in the continuation of large estates. Local examples include the Ilchester estate that has land in several locations (for instance much of Abbotsbury), to smaller parish-level examples such as the Littlebredy estate. The estate par excellence must be the Duchy of Cornwall that owns not only the Poundbury development but much other land around the town.

The landscape of the South Winterborne valley near Winterborne Came.

Hedgerows in the Piddle valley just south of Piddlehinton.

Such estates often encouraged the continuation of more traditional styles of farming, and are one of the reasons why the countryside round Dorchester retains many of its old field systems and hedgerows. Nevertheless, some areas have gone over to the large-scale mechanised farming that produces high crop yields.

Increasing mechanisation has not only meant the removal of some hedgerows. It also dramatically lessened the number of people working on the land, perhaps to the extent that this figure is now at its lowest since farming was introduced to this country some six thousand years ago. Thomas Hardy's novels catalogue the old way of life when there were people working all over the countryside – today you can walk for miles and only meet other hikers.

Towards the end of the century, similar views that had led to the restoration of heathland had an impact on farming. Landowners were increasingly being encouraged to manage their land in a way that made the landscape

Large-scale arable farming with rape in flower in the Frome valley east of Dorchester.

attractive for both visitors and wildlife, with hedgerow replanting being given grant-aid under the Countryside Stewardship scheme, for instance.

Gravel has been extracted from the Frome valley since time immemorial, and several small-scale operations were in progress in the early years of the century, notably around Warmwell area. Then planning permission for the large-scale work at Warmwell (much of it on the site of the Second World War airfield) was granted in the 1960s and site has been quarried ever since. Quarrying near West Knighton was granted consent in the late 1970s, and by the turn of the century had expanded towards West Stafford. Planning permissions for quarrying in the latter part of the century required that land was restored after quarrying finished.

The Hardy Monument is a major local landmark, and was constructed on the Ridgeway south-west of Dorchester in 1844 as a monument to the Admiral Hardy who Nelson wished to be kissed by. A car park was built here in the twentieth century, and it is visited for its views and as a starting point for walks, especially along the Ridgeway and the inland stretch of the South West Coast Path.

A quarry near Crossways.

Hardy's Monument, 1950.

Signpost at Dark Lane between Puddle-town and Tincleton.

Signpost at the central crossroads in Tincleton.

The survival of old-style signposts such as those above is a deliberate continuation of tradition. Many people see them as a characteristic of the Dorset countryside, and the County Council recognises their value and maintains rather than replaces them.

– 9 –
Villages Around Dorchester

*I*n this section I have tried to confine myself to those villages that are within 5 or 6 miles of Dorchester, but I see no reason not to break this rule if there is a worthwhile point to be made. At first glance, some of these villages can appear timeless, or at least not to have changed much for centuries, but a little bit of research or just a closer look soon shows that they underwent plenty of changes during the twentieth century.

New housing developments were a common feature of local villages in the later twentieth century. Some of this was to provide better accommodation for the existing inhabitants. The development of other settlements reflected their popularity for retirement or as places from which to commute to Dorchester or further afield. Charminster, which is only a couple of miles from Dorchester, is a good example – it lost some of its older buildings but still has enough of them to retain its charm, while developments on the edge of the village have greatly increased its size. It is interesting to see how attitudes to these developments have changed, and this is a matter that relates to how people perceive villages, as I shall try to explain.

Firstly, thatched cottages underwent fluctuations in popularity through the century. In 1906 the writer and retired doctor Frederick Treves (better-known for his study of Joseph Merrick, the 'Elephant Man') wrote fondly of Dorset's 'ancient villages of thatched roofs and rose-covered walls'. He and other early-twentieth-century writers and tourists who travelled the county may have liked them, but they did not have to live in them.

Cottages tended to be draughty, and a passage in Thomas Hardy's *Under the Greenwood Tree,* where during preparations for the final wedding people upstairs in a house are having conversations with those downstairs through the gaps in the floor, rather makes the point. The thatch often leaked, and needed to be replaced at intervals, which was an expensive business. The structure needed other repairs, as can be seen at Thomas Hardy's birthplace (see Chapter 6) where there are all sorts of patched repairs on the walls.

These factors, together with a view that such buildings were old-fashioned and 'progress' was necessary, meant that in the early to middle years of the century, many cottages were pulled down or, as happened a lot in Martinstown for instance, had their thatched roofs replaced by slate or tile.

However, Treves' views became more widespread as the century advanced. More people found leisure time to spend in the countryside and townspeople began retiring to the type of thatched cottage they had dreamed of.

So, while up until the 1980s or so, new houses built in the villages followed modern trends and often looked the same as buildings anywhere in the country, there was a change from around the early to mid-1990s. Around then, increased demand for traditional-style housing meant that many new properties in local villages were constructed in this manner, often with thatched roofs.

Much of this change has been put down to the influence of the Poundbury development and the new properties are sometimes referred as being in the 'Poundbury' style, but architects will dispute this, saying they have been working on similar lines independently. The properties in question are often traditional on the outside only, for modern facilities are still expected by buyers and today no-one wishes to hold direct conversations between bedroom and living room (except perhaps on a mobile 'phone).

Here are some examples in Bradford Peverell, which lies some 3 miles north-west of Dorchester on the side of the Frome valley. They are the work

Yew Tree Lane, Bradford Peverell.

Manor Lane, Bradford Peverell.

of David Wren, architect, and Raymond Eversden, builder, both of whom are Bradford Peverell residents. The Manor Lane development began in 1994, that at Yew Tree Lane was a little earlier. They are typical of developments that attempt to fit in with or recreate the feel of an historic village, using a mix of building materials such as flint, stone, brick and cob, together with roofs of thatch mixed with others of slate.

Another example can be found in the next village up the Frome valley, Stratton. An extensive development at the western end of the village began in the last years of the twentieth century and continued into the twenty-first. Called the Saxonfield development, it includes a new village green, village hall and a new pub, the Saxon Arms.

The latter is intended to be a community pub for the whole village, which is particularly important since the only other such establishment had closed previously. It is a Free House that now functions as both a village pub and

The Saxon Arms and the parish church in Stratton, seen from across the new village green.

a place to eat for visitors from further afield, particularly Dorchester. The building is constructed mainly of flint with courses of sandstone, and with brick used for the chimney, porch, bay windows and an 'extension'. The roof is thatched. The pub, the village hall that is just across the way from it, and the rather older parish church that forms the pub's backdrop, make an attractive group.

Now to look at some aspects of the twentieth century in individual villages.

BROADMAYNE

The historic centre of Broadmayne was along the Dorchester to Wareham road, but during the twentieth century development also spread out, some of it along the road that links Broadmayne with West Knighton, a mile or

Old Brickfields, Broadmayne.

so to the north. The name of one of the roads in this area, Old Brickfields, records what was here before the modern houses, for the road was built in what had been the main quarry of the clay used in making Broadmayne bricks.

This industry was at its height in the nineteenth century, but it continued into the twentieth before petering out after the First World War. Many buildings in the general area, including quite a few in Dorchester and Weymouth, are made from these bricks, whose colours are a range of lighter browns (but never red), often with black speckles – the latter means that they were sometimes called Broadmayne speckled bricks. The Corn Exchange is one of the best examples of their use in Dorchester.

Broadmayne brick in situ.

BRIANTSPUDDLE

Of the various Piddle/Puddle villages, Briantspuddle is the furthest down-stream of any size, and rarely has the appearance of a village been so influenced by one person.

In 1914 Sir Ernest Debenham, a wealthy London draper, bought four farms in Briantspuddle and began developing them. In the period after the First World War and up to 1932 he continued and also built nearly 50 cottages. His new buildings were constructed using locally-made traditional materials – cob, thatch and brick – but he was not averse to using rather more modern concrete as well. Many are in a very romantic Arts and Crafts style with some grand and unusual features never found on the cottage or work-place of the average Dorset farmhand. They mix with older cottages in what must have been a much smaller hamlet beforehand.

Sir Ernest's plan was to help reverse the population shift into towns by provid-ing good quality housing and to demonstrate that Great Britain could feed itself without needing imports (a point of some urgency after U-Boat attacks on British shipping in the Great War and which would be equally valid in the Second World War). Hence, his estate had a wide variety of activities such as forestry and bee-keeping. Sadly perhaps, the experiment did not survive his death in 1952, after which the estate was broken up.

Debenham was a cousin of Neville Chamberlain, Prime Minister at the outbreak of the Second World War, who sometimes stayed with him in Dorset for holidays.

Here is a selection of buildings associated with Sir Ernest.

The Ring is Sir Ernest's masterpiece, so don't miss it if you ever come to Briantspuddle! It was built around 1920 as the part of the estate's main dairy, although it is now four houses. A near-symmetrical structure extends around three sides of a green open space. A single-storey range faces out towards the village street, flanked by octagonal corner turrets that were used for cheesemaking, with large two-storey projecting wings on either side. The undulating roof is covered in thatch, and although it may not look like it, the walls are concrete blocks.

Bladen Valley is an avenue of housing at the west end of the village which was built around 1920 by Debenham, and shows him putting his theory into practice. These are large cottages (detached, semi-detached and in terraces of three) so that his tenants here lived in spacious conditions while the generous gardens gave them the chance to grow fruit and vegetables if they wished. There is little uniformity here – the mostly thatched cottages are in a variety of shapes, many of which would do the front of a chocolate box proud.

Part of The Ring.

A cottage at Bladen Valley.

The War Memorial.

At the entrance to Bladen Valley stands what at first sight looks like a market cross. In reality it is a memorial to the local dead of the First World War, carved by Eric Gill (1882-1940), a renowned sculptor, engraver and type designer, whose other work includes The Stations Of The Cross in Westminster Cathedral. On top of four steps there is a tall shaft surmounted by a small cross. On one side is a very modern-looking figure of Christ and on the opposite a Madonna and Child. There are twelve niches around the base, ten of which each have the name and details of one of the dead, and above them is a quotation from Mother Julian of Norwich, a medieval mystic. This quotation, which is beginning to be lost under lichen, reads 'It is sooth that sin is cause of all the pain but all shall be well and all shall be well and all manner of things shall be well'.

CHARMINSTER

Later twentieth century developments in and around the village have brought new life into Charminster rather than destroying its character. The occupants were undoubtedly attracted by the easy access to Dorchester, and many came to work at the old Herrison Hospital just outside the village. A very attractive and extensive historic centre survives, of which the church is the centrepiece.

Postcard of Charminster church – an early-twentieth-century view.

Courtesy Dorset Local History Centre

The Three Compasses Inn is a good example of an early-twentieth-century pub. It was built in 1916, although there has been an inn of the same name here for much longer. The name came from the nearby junction, where three routes coming from the north, west and east met. A road heading to the south was added to the junction in the eighteenth century to link to the new turnpike that took the Dorchester to Yeovil road around Charminster – this now forms part of the A350.

The Three Compasses Inn.

The large car park in front of the building is built on land once occupied by a blacksmith's forge and a brewhouse belonging to the inn. While the pub's skittle alley is now at the back, it was originally in a room above the bar, which must have made a quiet pint into something of a rarity!

Today the only retailing businesses in Charminster are the village shop shown below and two pubs – the Three Compasses Inn and the Inn for All Seasons (although the Sun Inn at Burton is also in the parish). Comparison with the 1903 Kelly's trade directory entry for Charminster shows just how many businesses the village lost over the course of the twentieth century. It lists two pub landlords, two beer retailers, a shopkeeper, a miller, a watchmaker, a grocer, two bakers, a butcher, a carpenter, and a combined butcher and grocer who would have fallen foul of today's Health and Safety regulations, as well as various people employed in building and agricultural trades that may not have needed shops. Charminster is probably not exceptional in the number of businesses it lost.

Charminster's village shop and Post Office.

Courtesy Dorset Local History Centre

Postcard of Charminster – the bridge across the River Cerne. Note the delivery boy in this Edwardian view, presumably sent out by a local business.

Courtesy the Herbert Collection

Dorset Roads, probably 1950s. The junction of the A350 with the A37 just south of Charminster. Both roads date from the eighteenth century.

The turnpike taking the Dorchester to Yeovil route (the present A37) that was constructed in the eighteenth century bypassed Charminster to the south.

St Mary's, Charminster, early twentieth century, showing the right of way along the Cerne.

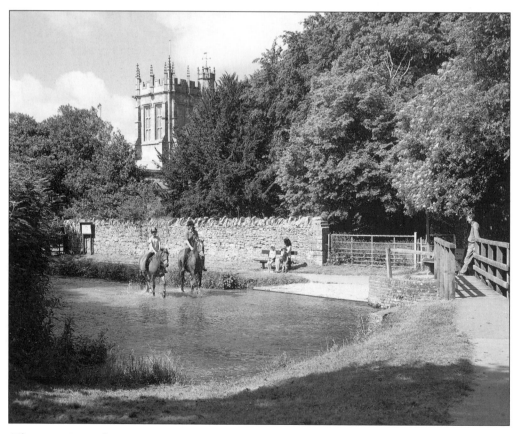

The same view today.

Before then, the village street was the main road. To avoid the steep East Hill, carts and the like sometimes used Mill Lane as an alternative route, going along a shallow stretch of the River Cerne, termed a 'long ford', as a link to the village street. To make this stretch easier to 'navigate', the riverbed here was paved with stone, some of which can still be seen today. The stretch is still technically a road.

Charminster is a good example of the efforts that are being made to give villages back their character and sense of community, much of which can be lost with the withdrawal of facilities.

Miller's Community Orchard.

Mill Lane has already been mentioned, and another lane that bears the same name runs off it north at right angles. On the corner between the two, there is Miller's Community Orchard, recently planted with traditional Dorset varieties of apple tree, and with seating to enjoy the sight. The north-bearing Mill Lane runs out to Prince's Plot, a picnic and nature area that runs up the side of the valley and that belongs to Charminster Parish Council. Popular opinion is that Prince's Plot has a royal connection, perhaps having been donated by the Prince of Wales. In fact, Prince was the name of a locally-noted shire horse, often exhibited at the Dorchester show, who lived here thirty or forty years ago.

Charlton Down.

Much of what had been the Herrison Hospital closed down in the 1990s and the site was redeveloped for housing under the name Charlton Down.

CERNE ABBAS

Cerne Abbas must be Dorset's tourist village par excellence. It is full of very attractive old buildings, has historic features such as the Cerne Abbas Giant and the remains of a medieval abbey. Its setting is superb, beside the River Cerne in the well-wooded valley of the same name.

These two early-twentieth century views below show what the village was like before tourism had an impact. It was just an ordinary Dorset village, and everything looks more basic and in places somewhat run-down.

The tourist hot-spot of Cerne Abbas.

Long Street, Cerne Abbas.

Abbey Street, Cerne Abbas.

For comparison, here are two views from the 1960s.

Courtesy the Herbert Collection

Courtesy the Herbert Collection

Cerne Abbas 9/2/62.   Two views, one looking south down Abbey Street and the one looking west towards the back of the Royal Oak.

CROSSWAYS AND WARMWELL

Many military airfields were hurriedly established in the early days of the Second World War. One was known as Warmwell airfield, and lay north of that village towards Crossways. Despite poor accommodation and complaints about poor facilities provided by civilian suppliers, it served its purpose well. During the Battle of Britain it was the base for 609 Squadron, being bombed on 25 August 1940, but with only limited damage.

By March 1944 the Royal Air Force had largely moved away, although an air-sea rescue squadron remained, and three squadrons of P38J Lockheed Lightnings of the United States Air Force moved in as part of the D-Day preparations. The Normandy invasion operations were supported from here, until the advance of the Allies began to leave Warmwell too far in the rear. By September, the American squadrons had relocated to bases in liberated parts of France.

Although the airfield has gone, there are reminders in Crossways village. One is a memorial, located off Mount Skippet Way, that was dedicated on 11 June 1989 to all who lost their lives while serving at the airfield. Another is Crossways village hall, which began life as the airfield's cinema.

The site of Warmwell airfield, much of which has since been quarried.

The memorial in Crossways.

Crossways village hall.

Until the Second World War, Crossways lived up to its name, consisting of a few houses around a junction of roads and lanes. Afterwards, 'Dig for Victory' plots were sold here. These were small areas of land on which the buyers could build themselves a bungalow. In the 1950s, surviving airfield buildings were used as a lodging camp for the construction crew working on the Winfrith nuclear power station over towards Wool.

Crossways then continued to grow in a more planned fashion, partly intended to serve as a dormitory for workers at the new power station. When this facility did not develop as intended, the place instead became home for a number of people who commuted to work in places like Dorchester and Weymouth. Its expanding population still lacks some facilities, and construction of a school is planned.

Crossways.

GODMANSTONE

Godmanstone lies a couple of miles south of Cerne Abbas down the Cerne valley. It is home to the Smith's Arms, which lays claim to the title of 'England's smallest pub'.

These two views look towards the Smith's Arms. The modern one has the River Cerne running across the foreground in a narrow channel with the pub's garden beyond. The older photograph shows the river spreading across a wider area to form a pond, so reclamation work much have taken place in the intervening period.

The Smiths Arms, Godman-stone, before 1922.

Courtesy Dorset Local History Centre

The Smiths Arms today.

MARTINSTOWN

Martinstown, a couple of miles south-west of Dorchester, is a good example of a village with a number of twentieth-century developments. Since the village lies in the narrow valley of the South Winterborne, many of these were infill developments, i.e. within the existing area of the village rather than outside it. Also, many of the old thatched cottages were given slate roofs – making them less attractive for visitors, but more pleasant to live in with less maintenance. These two factors brought people in and helped to keep the village alive – so it still has a pub and a village shop, unlike many other villages.

Courtesy the Herbert Collection

Martinstown 29/4/82.

Hardy Close was the first of the private modern developments in the village, dating from the 1960s. Previously the site had been a field, and during the Second World War an army camp was set up here, which was in turn converted to hold prisoners-of-war, the last of whom were repatriated in 1947. Before that, the field was often used as the site for Martinstown Fair, held every year on 23 November and a highlight of the village year. The sale of sheep and other livestock was the principal economic reason for the fair, but this was also a social gathering.

Later-twentieth-century houses in Martinstown.

MORETON

Moreton is a small village 6 miles east of Dorchester in the Frome valley. It has a very attractive Georgian church, built in 1776 by James Frampton of Moreton House.

In the Second World War the church was hit by a bomb, as shown opposite. The destroyed windows were replaced over the next few decades by a superb series of engraved windows – the work of Lawrence Whistler. They depict a variety of subjects, ranging from Second World War aircraft to a galaxy.

The church attracts visitors to Moreton, as does the grave of T. E. Lawrence, better known as Lawrence of Arabia. He lived at Clouds Hill nearby, and was killed in a motorcycle accident in 1935. His funeral was attended by many notables, including Winston Churchill.

Moreton church 2/6/61.

Courtesy the Herbert Collection

Details of war damage, 1941.

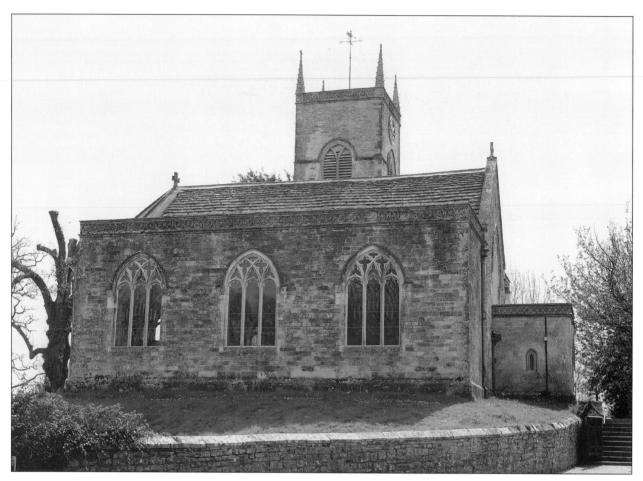

Moreton church today.

Moreton church window by Whistler, 4/12/72.

Moreton cemetery, wherein Lawrence is buried.

Lawrence's grave.

Lawrence's funeral 1935 – note Winston Churchill on the left in the bottom photo.

Old houses, Moreton 1910.

Moreton. The school.

The village school has now closed and was recently converted into a teashop
The two views below were taken from opposite ends of the village street.

Courtesy the Herbert Collection

Moreton. The street.

Moreton. The village street and cottages in Moreton today.

Here are two views, separated by about a century, of this footbridge over the Frome on the edge of Moreton.

The Long Bridge, Moreton c.1910.

The Long Bridge.

PIDDLETRENTHIDE

The River Piddle runs on a similar course a few miles to the north of the Frome. A series of villages and smaller settlements along the Piddle's valley bear its name, such as Piddletrenthide which is the furthest upstream, while sensibilities of recent centuries about the word Piddle have changed that part of some of their names to the more socially-acceptable Puddle. Thus we talk of the Tolpuddle Martyrs rather than those of Tolpiddle.

Piddletrenthide's manor house was built in the late eighteenth century. The upper storey was added in 1832.

Piddletrenthide is a long village, strung out along the road that runs down the Piddle valley.

Piddletrenthide.

Courtesy Maureen Attwooll

Manor House, early twentieth century.

Courtesy Dorset Local History Centre

Middle Tything, Piddletrenthide. No. 2, 1930s.

PUDDLETOWN

Many villages around Dorchester have lost their village pub. Puddletown has lost two. The one shown in the upper illustration here, the Kings Arms, was on the south side of the main junction, and has been replaced by housing.

The Prince of Wales closed in the early years of the twenty-first century.

High Street, Puddletown – 1920s or 1930s.

The Prince of Wales pub in 1969.

Courtesy the Herbert Collection

A view of the central junction in Puddletown dating from 1969.

Courtesy Dorset Local History Centre

Blandford Road, Puddletown – 1920s or 1930s.

The Blue Vinney today.

The above two pictures are comparative views of Puddletown's third and surviving pub, the Blue Vinney.

Many of the buildings in Puddletown were built in the late nineteenth century by John Brymer, who bought Ilsington House and thus became lord of the manor at Puddletown. These included the Reading Room, built in 1870. Col Brymer was John's son.

The Reading Room, with the church tower in the background, 1969.

Ilsington House and Col W. E. Brymer, c.1905.

Courtesy Maureen Attwooll

SYDLING ST NICHOLAS

Sydling St Nicholas lies some 6 miles north-west of Dorchester as the crow flies (rather further for those who have to use the roads) in the Sydling valley. Here are two similar views of East Street, taken some seventy years apart. Some of the details have changed (for instance, the little bridge has been rebuilt), but the general appearance is still there.

Courtesy Dorset Local History Centre

Postcard of Sydling, early 1930s.

Sydling St Nicholas — a contemporary view.

TINCLETON

Clyffe House was built by the architect Benjamin Ferrey in 1842 (he also built Tincleton's parish church and probably the village school). The upper photograph looks from the south, and a gardener's cottage is to the right of the main house. The estate of which this house was the centre broke up in the inter-war years, and after the Second World War the house passed to Dorset County Council and latterly became flats. The gardens in the foreground are fields under cultivation today.

Like many villages, Tincleton has lost its local shop. The former Post Office and stores closed in the 1980s.

Clyffe House, Tincleton – early twentieth century.

Courtesy Maureen Attwooll

The Old Post Office, Tincleton.

TOLPUDDLE

1934 was an important year in Tolpuddle, for it was the centenary of the trial of the Tolpuddle Martyrs. In the early 1830s, agricultural labourers were receiving lower wages, the cost of foodstuffs was rising, and newly-introduced threshing machines were cutting the amount of work available. Unrest among these people was causing concern to the authorities around the country. In 1833, labourers in Tolpuddle formed a trade union with the aim of obtaining better wages, swearing an oath as they did so. The six ring-leaders (Thomas Standfield and his son John, James Hammett, James Brine and the brothers George and James Loveless) were arrested on a rather 'dodgy' charge relating to the administering of the oath, since forming a trade union was perfectly legal. They were tried in the Dorchester Crown Court in Shire Hall on 17 March 1834 and sentenced to transportation.

A public outcry resulted from the men's treatment, and eventually the Tolpuddle Martyrs, as they became known, were brought back from Australia to a public welcome.

The almshouses in Tolpuddle.

The Martyrs remain in high esteem today, and the Trades Union Congress still holds a rally in Tolpuddle every July to commemorate them. In 1934 the T.U.C. built almshouses in the village for the centenary celebrations. One room in these almshouses now has a display on the Martyrs.

In the same year, Sir Ernest Debenham of Briantspuddle erected a commemorative shelter on Tolpuddle village green, where the meeting to form the union was held.

The shelter on the village green.

TOLPUDDLE COTTAGES.

Courtesy Maureen Attwooll

Tolpuddle Cottages, pre-1934. This shows the green before the shelter was built.

Shire Hall in Dorchester. The scene of the Martyrs' trial now has a display on that event.

WEST KNIGHTON

West Knighton school was built in 1865 in Victorian Gothic style, replacing an earlier school in the upper floor of what is now Steps Cottage on the opposite side of the village street. It was replaced in turn when Broadmayne First School was built to serve the two villages.

Today, the building is a pair of properties called the Old School House and the Old School, the former being the master's house originally. There is a datestone inscribed 'HB 1865' on a front gable of the Old School House, while the Old School still has a clock in the gable of the porch – there must have been no excuse for latecomers.

West Knighton school c.1920.

Courtesy the Herbert Collection

WEST STAFFORD

Not that much has changed in this part of West Stafford, a village that is a couple of miles east of Dorchester in the Frome valley. The street has been given a tarmac surface as you might expect, there is a new house behind the church and a few aerials here and there.

Courtesy Dorset Local History Centre

An early-twentieth-century view of the village street in West Stafford.

The same view today.

WHITCOMBE

Whitcombe lies a couple of miles south-east of Dorchester beside the road to Wareham. It is a picturesque place that lies in a natural bowl and has an assemblage of thatched eighteenth-century cottages. It survives in this fine condition because of the care and co-operation of landowners and the authorities.

The best-known feature is the medieval parish church, which is slightly detached from the rest of the settlement, among earthworks that are the remains of the medieval village and which are protected as a Scheduled Ancient Monument. Inside the church there is a fifteenth-century wall-painting of St Christopher carrying a child (who in the story turns out to be Christ) across a river.

Courtesy Maureen Attwooll

Whitcombe church c.1907.

The same view today. Note how the ivy has gone. It may be attractive, but its roots can be extremely damaging to a structure such as this tower.

Came Church, near Dorchester.

Winterborne Came church c.1910.

WINTERBORNE CAME

Note the ivy on the church tower in the photograph above, just as there is in the old photograph of Whitcombe church. This is no longer there, perhaps because of concern about the damage its roots can cause.

Winterborne Came is one of a string of villages that lie along the valley of the South Winterborne River, which loops around to the south of Dorchester. Today it consists of the church, Came House (an eighteenth-century manor house) and a few cottages only. The parish church once served several other villages in the valley, but these villages have largely disappeared. It was thus almost a typical example of a common occurrence of the twentieth century, when a small congregation led to a church being declared redundant. In this case, though, the church remains in occasional use because in 1989 it was given into the care of what is today called The Churches Conservation Trust. This maintains the building, in its own words 'for the benefit of this and future generations' and has carried out repairs since it took it over.

Apart form its attractiveness, one of the reasons why this church is cared for in this way must be that the Dorset dialect poet William Barnes (1801-86) was rector here for the last twenty-four years of his life and is buried in the churchyard. His grave, marked by a Celtic cross with intertwined animals that must be evidence of his antiquarian interest, is the tallest monument in the graveyard and also among the best tended.

WINTERBORNE FARRINGDON

A little to the west of Winterborne Came there is all that remains of another Winterborne village. Winterborne Farringdon was declining in population at the end of the Middle Ages, but struggled on for a few centuries. The earthworks of the old village are still there and in the twentieth century they were protected as a Scheduled Ancient Monument. The single wall that remains standing in the middle belonged to the parish church, the rest of which was taken away for reuse in the days before old churches were thought worthy of conservation.

Winterborne Farringdon seen from the road through the South Winterborne valley.

WINTERBORNE HERRINGSTON

And finally, here are two comparative views, taken a century apart, of the approach to the great house known simply as Herringston. The north front that is seen in these photographs dates from the early nineteenth century, but much of the house dates from the reign of Elizabeth I. Other than this house, Winterborne Herringston is almost another deserted settlement.

Winterborne Herringston c.1904.

Winterborne Herringston today.

Courtesy Dorset Local History Centre

Further Reading

This is not a complete bibliography of every work consulted in writing this book; rather it is a list that the reader might find helpful in seeking other books on Dorchester and related topics discussed in this work

Bartelot, R.G., 1915, *The History of Fordington*, Henry Ling, Dorchester.

Cullingford, C.N., 1980, *A History of Dorset*, Phillimore.

Draper, J., 2001, *Dorchester Past*, Phillimore.

Draper, J., 1986, *Dorset, The Complete Guide*, The Dovecote Press.

Forty, G., 1994, *Frontline Dorset, A County at War 1939-45*, Dorset Books.

Hardy, T., 1872, *Under the Greenwood Tree*, Macmillan and Co. Ltd.

Hawkes, J., 1982, *Mortimer Wheeler – Adventurer in Archaeology*, Weidenfeld and Nicolson.

Gosling, T., 1994, *Dorchester in Old Photographs*, Alan Sutton Publishing Ltd.

Kelly's Directories, 1903, *Dorsetshire*.

Kingston Maurward Association, 2000, *Celebrating the First Fifty Years*, Kingston Maurward Association.

McGee, C., 2001, *Around Dorchester*, The Francis Frith Collection.

Mee, A.(ed.), 1939, *Dorset - Thomas Hardy's Country*, Hodder and Stoughton.

Murphy, J., 1979, *Dorset at War*, Dorset Publishing Company.

Oakley, M., 2001, *Railway Stations*, Discover Dorset Series, The Dovecote Press.

H.R.H. The Prince of Wales, 1989, *A Vision of Britain*.

Putnam, B., undated, *The Roman Town House at Dorchester*, Dorset County Council.

Sharples, N.M., 1991, *Maiden Castle Excavations and field survey 1985-6*, Historic Buildings & Monuments

Commission for England Report no. 19.

Treves, F., 1906, *Highways and Byways of Dorset*, Macmillan & Co. Ltd.

Wallis, S., 2004, *Dorchester – A History and Celebration*, Frith Book Company Ltd.

Wheeler, R.E.M., 1943, *Maiden Castle, Dorset*, Rep. Res. Comm. Soc. Antiq. London 11.

Woodward, P.J., Davies, S.M. & Graham, A.H., 1993, *Excavations at the old Methodist Chapel and Greyhound Yard, Dorchester, 1981-4*, Dorset Natural History and Archaeological Society Monograph no. 12.